DIVING **DEEP**

EXPERIENCING JESUS THROUGH
SPIRITUAL Disciplines

STUDENT JOURNAL

AMY SIMPSON

Loveland, Colorado

Diving Deep Student Journal
Experiencing Jesus Through Spiritual Disciplines
Copyright © 2002 Amy Simpson

Visit our Web site: **www.grouppublishing.com**

Credits
Editor: Kelli B. Trujillo
Creative Development Editor: Dave Thornton
Chief Creative Officer: Joani Schultz
Copy Editor: Lyndsay E. Bierce
Art Directors: Sharon Anderson, Julia Ryan
Cover Art Director: Jeff A. Storm
Cover Designer: Julia Ryan
Computer Graphic Artist: Joyce Douglas
Cover Photographer: Blanca Middlebrook
Production Manager: Dodie Tipton

Unless otherwise noted, Scripture taken from the HOLY BIBLE,
NEW INTERNATIONAL VERSION®. Copyright © 1973, 1978, 1984 by International
Bible Society. Used by permission of Zondervan Publishing House. All rights reserved.

ISBN 0-7644-2388-6

10 9 8 7 6 5 4 3 2   11 10 09 08 07 06 05 04 03 02
Printed in the United States of America.

This journal belongs to: This journal belongs to: This journal belongs to: This journal belongs to: This journal belongs to: This journal belongs to:

CONTENTS

SPIRITUAL DISCIPLINES LIST

WORSHIP

Worship is proclaiming the truth, either to ourselves or to others, about who God is and what God does.

SOLITUDE

Solitude is spending time alone with God, away from the distractions and distortions of being with others.

FELLOWSHIP

Fellowship is being with others in ways that help us grow in our faith: encouraging people, reminding them who God is, and building their faith.

SERVICE

Service is humbly giving of ourselves and expecting nothing in return.

CONFESSION

Confession is telling the truth about what we've done and admitting our responsibility so we can experience true forgiveness.

SUBMISSION

Submission is giving up our way in favor of someone else's.

FASTING

Fasting is purposely depriving ourselves of things that can keep us from depending on God to meet our needs.

CELEBRATION

Celebration is focusing on God's work in the world, affirming and drawing strength from the joys of life and eternity.

STUDY

Study is using any tools available to learn all we can about the truth of God's Word.

SILENCE

Silence is being silent or shutting out sounds so we can hear God's voice and get to know him better.

SACRIFICE

Sacrifice is giving until it hurts and offering your life as a gift to God.

PRAYER

Prayer is communicating with God to help us know God, hear from God, and express dependence on God.

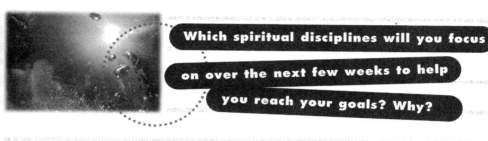

Which spiritual disciplines will you focus on over the next few weeks to help you reach your goals? Why?

For some early Christians commonly called the desert fathers, spiritual discipline was a way of life. These men were monks who gave up everything they had, turned their backs on civilization as they knew it, and chose to live a hard life in the desert. Among the most well-known of these desert fathers were St. Antony and Pachomius.

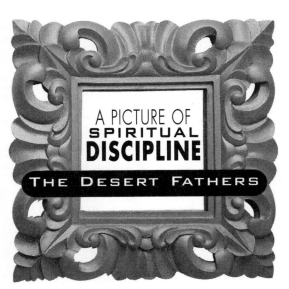

A PICTURE OF
SPIRITUAL
DISCIPLINE
THE DESERT FATHERS

Every element of daily life for the desert fathers was crafted specifically to obey God's Word. They spent their days in disciplines that would help them grow spiritually: meditating on Scripture, praying, memorizing the Bible, seeking guidance from the wise among them, living on a simple diet, and denying sexual desires.

The desert fathers became pillars in the Christian community. They reintegrated with society and became invaluable in many ways. Because they had no property or biases of their own, they often settled quarrels. They performed miracles, counseled government officials, and worshipped in the nearest churches. The strength they drew from their disciplined life gave them the opportunity to minister to many people and to advance the growth of the Christian church.

SPIRITUAL

RESPONDING TO **GOD**

Write to God about some spiritual goals you'd like to meet in the next week, year, five years, and ten years.

DISCIPLINE

SPIRITUAL

attention, and then to listen for the word of God as it moves from our head

DISCIPLINE

For the Christian band Third Day, making music isn't about winning fans or getting rich. It's about worship. But worship doesn't happen just when they're making music. To Third Day, worship is a lifestyle.

"You can worship God while walking down the street. You can worship God while washing dishes or at your job. Worship is bringing God to the center of whatever you're doing," says guitarist Brad Avery.

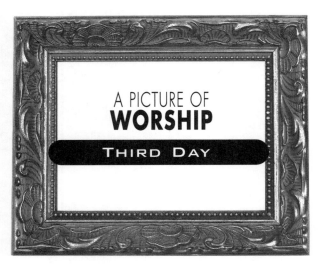

Although Third Day has experienced great success with their music, they play their music to worship God, to proclaim truth about who God is and what he does. They see music as a mission. They want to share Jesus through their songs. This mission is an extension of what they believe their lives should be about.

Bassist Tai Anderson says, "If you took music away, I believe every guy in this band would find another way to serve God."

WORSHIP

RESPONDING TO GOD

Write your own psalm of praise to God, using Psalm 103 as your model. Make it personal to your experiences with God. Be sure to include proclamations of who God is, what God does, how God has changed your life, and where you stand in relationship to God.

WORSHIP

being ablaze with a desire for God."—Os Guinness

For Christian musician Michelle Tumes, solitude is an important part of knowing God. Growing up in Australia, Michelle spent a lot of time on lonely, secluded beaches. As she spent time alone with God, she would think about her relationship with God and experience God's presence through the beauty of nature around her.

A PICTURE OF
SOLITUDE
MICHELLE TUMES

Through these times with God, Michelle has experienced great peace in her life. And she tries to share that peace with others through her music. She's always been an introvert. She says, "I'm more concerned with developing what's on the inside. And ultimately, that means learning to sit quietly and listen to the voice of God. I would often sit where the waves rolled in upon the sand and pray there." She tries to produce that same kind of experience in her music. Her goal is to help others find peaceful interaction with God.

SOLITUDE

RESPONDING TO GOD

Consider these questions and write your thoughts.

- **Who or what in your life most distracts you from a Christ-like perspective?**

- **How can times of solitude help you minimize the influence of this distraction?**

DIVING DEEP

SOLITUDE

place...we always carry with us a portable sanctuary of the heart."

—Richard Foster

Acts 2:42-47 and 4:32-35 give us a picture of life among the early Christians. Both of these passages describe the importance of fellowship in their spiritual experience.

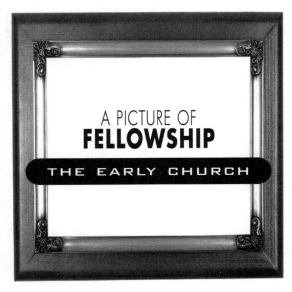

These early Christians didn't just come together for worship once a week; they shared their lives with one another. They prayed together, ate together, invited one another into their homes, and shared money to help one another. They met together at the temple every day to worship.

The Scripture implies that this fellowship had great power in their lives. These early Christians saw many wonders and miracles among them. They worshipped God with sincerity, and they attracted many new Christians by their lifestyle.

FELLOWSHIP

RESPONDING TO GOD

Write your answers to these questions:

- **Why do I need other Christians?**

- **What can I contribute to the body of Christ?**

- **How can I experience more true fellowship?**

"fellowship occurs, I believe, when there are *expressions of*

FELLOWSHIP

genuine Christianity freely shared among God's family members."—Charles

King David is widely considered to be the greatest king of ancient Israel. But he didn't get that reputation because he was perfect. He earned that reputation by following God. Even before David was appointed king of Israel, the prophet Samuel called him "a man after [God's] own heart" (1 Samuel 13:14).

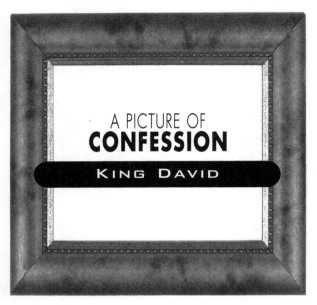

When David fell into serious sin by committing adultery with Bathsheba, he continued to pursue his relationship with God by confessing his sin. God sent the prophet Nathan to confront David with the facts of his sin. When confronted, David didn't try to deny what he had done. He simply said, "I have sinned against the Lord" (2 Samuel 12:13).

Through confession, David welcomed God's presence and change in his life. In Psalm 139:23-24, he wrote, "Search me, O God, and know my heart; test me and know my anxious thoughts. See if there is any offensive way in me, and lead me in the way everlasting." Throughout the Psalms, David exhibited a profound sense of intimacy with God.

CONFESSION

RESPONDING TO **GOD**

Write a prayer of confession, exposing the raw, ugly truth about yourself. Write out everything you try to keep hidden about yourself—God knows it all anyway! Then rip, burn, or otherwise destroy the paper as a symbol of God's forgiveness.

CONFESSION

area in personal prayer today."—Bill Hybels

When Richard Foster entered church ministry, he was ambitious and eager to prove himself as a pastor. After three months of ministry at his first church, he was "spiritually bankrupt." He had given all he could to his congregation, and he had nothing left to offer.

Through various influences in Foster's life, he discovered the power of spiritual discipline. That discovery transformed his life and the lives of the people in his congregation.

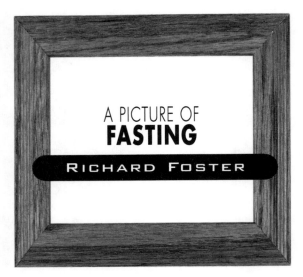

A PICTURE OF
FASTING

RICHARD FOSTER

One of the disciplines Foster practiced was the discipline of fasting. His experiences with fasting led him to discover his dependence on food. Foster says, "The first thing I learned about myself in experiences of fasting was my passion for good feelings. I was hungry and I did not feel good. All of a sudden I began to realize that I would do almost anything to feel good."

As Richard Foster experienced spiritual renewal through disciplines such as fasting, he was moved to write a book about the value of spiritual discipline. His book *Celebration of Discipline* has inspired many people for decades to initiate spiritual growth in their lives through discipline.

FASTING

RESPONDING TO **GOD**

Tell God about your needs, and be very specific. Ask God to meet those needs and to help you avoid the temptation to try to meet those needs in other ways.

"No matter what life gives us, we always want more. Our

FASTING

craving for things never sleeps long enough to allow us peace."—Calvin

At age twelve, Agnes Gonxha Bojaxhiu of Albania sensed God calling her to serve him. She accepted that call and eventually became Mother Teresa of Calcutta. While she was a teacher at a convent school, she experienced a second, more specific calling from God: to give up everything and serve the "poorest of the poor."

A PICTURE OF **SERVICE**

MOTHER TERESA

So Mother Teresa followed God's calling on her life. She began a new order of nuns to minister to the poor, sick, and dying. She and the other nuns in her order cared for people by providing food, medical supplies, and loving presence. They tenderly bathed those under their care. They showed Jesus' love. According to Mother Teresa, "If our actions are just useful actions that give no joy to the people, our poor people would never be able to rise up to the call which we want them to hear, the call to come closer to God. We want to make them feel that they are loved."

Mother Teresa opened a home for dying and destitute people in Calcutta, India. Eventually, her ministry extended to five continents. Although she gained great recognition—even a Nobel Peace Prize—for her work around the world, Mother Teresa served for God alone.

SERVICE

RESPONDING TO GOD

Rewrite Luke 6:32-36 in your own words.

SERVICE

you: 'Every time you meet another human being you have the opportunity.'"

—Walter Wangerin Jr.

By most accounts, Martin Luther was a great man. While he was a law student in 1505, he had a life-changing experience with God and entered a monastery. Later he became a priest.

Over time, Luther became concerned about whether he was living up to God's standards for salvation. He studied the Bible and discovered in the writings of Paul that God's gift of salvation is just that—a gift. God grants us forgiveness, salvation, and eternal life as we put our faith in him. This message was personally freeing to Luther. But this message also went against what the church was teaching at that time. Many church leaders had become more focused on doing things for God than on what God has done for us.

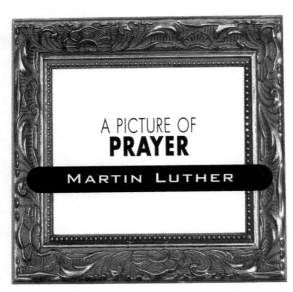

A PICTURE OF
PRAYER

MARTIN LUTHER

Luther spoke out against many of the messages being preached in the Christian church at that time. He challenged the church leaders of his day and sparked a reformation movement that changed the church. He translated Scripture into German, married, raised six children, worked to build an educational system, wrote a liturgy, crafted hymns, and put together two catechisms. He was a busy man.

But Martin Luther wasn't too busy to pray. In fact, prayer was the foundation of his great zeal. "I have so much business," he said, "I cannot get on without spending three hours daily in prayer." He also claimed, "He that has prayed well has studied well."

Martin Luther found his strength in prayer, and God used that strength to change the face of Christianity and western civilization.

PRAYER

RESPONDING TO GOD

Make a list of everyone and everything you want to pray for. Then work your way through the list, praying for each entry. If you sense God speaking to you during this time, pause and write down what you hear from God. When you've finished, spend some time in silence, listening for God's voice. Write down everything you sense from God. To practice prayer, you may want to continue to use this pattern to start and maintain an ongoing prayer journal.

PRAYER

corner of life...Prayer becomes an ongoing communication between a

Martin Luther King Jr. skipped two grades in school. He passed the entrance exam to Morehouse College by the time he was fifteen. While he was in college, he felt God calling him into ministry, through "an inner urge...to serve humanity."

After college, King attended seminary and Boston University, then became the pastor at Dexter Baptist Church in Montgomery, Alabama. He was just beginning his church ministry, but he had no idea how God would ultimately use him to minister to thousands.

A PICTURE OF
SACRIFICE

MARTIN LUTHER KING JR

In 1955, King became president of the newly formed Montgomery Improvement Association. He led the group in nonviolent protests of racial inequality, starting a long ministry of fighting for civil rights in America.

Throughout the late 1950s and most of the 1960s, Martin Luther King Jr. gave up his chances to live in comfortable anonymity. He followed God's calling on his life, putting his life at risk. He received death threats, was stoned, and was arrested several times, but he pressed on, proclaiming the message God had called him to proclaim, all the while showing Jesus' love by rejecting violence.

On April 4, 1968, Martin Luther King Jr. made the ultimate sacrifice: He was assassinated. He gave his life struggling for the dream God had given him.

SACRIFICE

RESPONDING TO GOD

Consider this question and write your thoughts.

- **Why does God give us great gifts and then ask us to sacrifice them?**

"God spilt the life of His Son that the world might be saved;

SACRIFICE

are we prepared to spill out our lives for Him?"—Oswald Chambers

John Wesley wanted to become a better person—more like Christ. He believed that studying God's Word was a great responsibility of the Christian. He also believed that studying God's Word would help him become more like Jesus. In his quest to do so, he studied the writings of a variety of Christian thinkers. He developed a great understanding of theology and Christian thought.

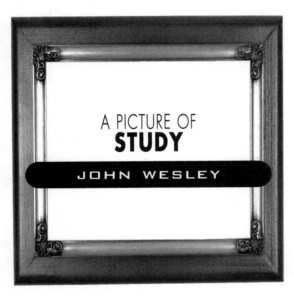

A PICTURE OF
STUDY

JOHN WESLEY

Along with his brother Charles, John Wesley founded the Methodist movement. And through his continued study, he helped keep the movement alive. He wrote hundreds of titles on spiritual issues, which were widely read. He published two biblical commentaries, including his own translation of the Bible from Greek into English. He used his writings to constantly encourage other Christians to live more righteous lives.

Because of John Wesley's discipline in study, many people began studying Scripture for themselves. And as a result, they followed God more closely.

STUDY

RESPONDING TO GOD

Write your answers to these questions:

- **What are your biggest questions about the Bible or the Christian faith?**

- **How might you get good answers to those questions?**

STUDY

you in a personal and real way."—Henry T. Blackaby

In the 1650s, John Bunyan was a popular preacher, speaking to large audiences in England. In 1660, the government declared it illegal to preach or hold a church service apart from the regulations of the Church of England. Bunyan didn't want to be controlled by the government because he believed God alone had called him to preach, so his preaching wasn't licensed by the Church of England. So Bunyan was put in jail for twelve years. Then a few years after his release, he was jailed for another six months.

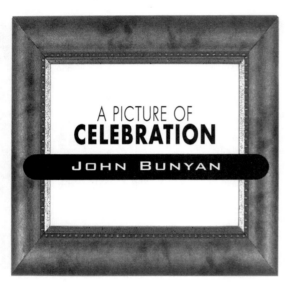

A PICTURE OF
CELEBRATION

JOHN BUNYAN

While Bunyan was in prison, he could have sulked, blamed God, and grown bitter. Instead, he chose to take up writing. He wrote religious tracts and pamphlets. He put together a spiritual autobiography, *Grace Abounding to the Chief of Sinners*. And he wrote the bulk of his famous work *The Pilgrim's Progress from This World to That Which Is to Come*. *The Pilgrim's Progress*, which would become the most widely read book in English except for the Bible, was an elaborate allegory of the journey through life with Christ.

Instead of focusing on his difficult circumstances, Bunyan chose to celebrate by reading the Bible and writing about God's great works in the lives of people. He later said, "I never knew all there was in the Bible until I spent those years in jail. I was constantly finding new treasures." In *The Pilgrim's Progress*, Bunyan wrote, "I would rather walk in the dark with God than go alone in the light." Bunyan's writings were celebrations of God's work in the lives of people and in his own life. And Bunyan's celebration has had a dramatic effect on the lives of people ever since.

CELEBRATION

RESPONDING TO GOD

Complete this prayer-starter: "God, here's what I want to celebrate in my life..."

CELEBRATION

pleasure—gathering with people we love, eating and drinking, singing and

dancing." —John Ortberg

Henri Nouwen was a successful man. He was trained as a psychologist and a theologian. He taught at Notre Dame, Yale, and Harvard. He was a sought-after writer and speaker. But something was missing. Part of him felt called to give up his achievements and successes and simply rest in knowing that he was God's beloved child.

A PICTURE OF
SUBMISSION

HENRI NOUWEN

In 1985, Henri Nouwen listened to that voice. He left behind the rigors of his schedule and all his success and became part of a community for developmentally disabled people at L'Arche Daybreak Community in Toronto. Nouwen was the resident priest in this community for ten years, willingly giving up his own desires to succeed and submitting to the needs of others. Nouwen spent two hours a day preparing Adam, one of the residents, for the day. He bathed Adam, shaved his face, brushed his teeth, combed his hair, and guided his hand as he ate breakfast.

In his experience at Daybreak, Nouwen learned from the residents. He developed a deep sense of humility. And in caring for Adam, he came to understand God's love more deeply than ever before.

SUBMISSION

RESPONDING TO GOD

Write your answers to these questions:

• What relationships in your life are causing you frustration?

• What would happen if you chose to submit to those people?

SUBMISSION

great."—Lawrence O. Richards

The Trappist monks live a disciplined life. The Trappists are a monastic order that originated in seventeenth-century France.

The Trappists have traditionally held to a vow of silence, although recently some Trappist monasteries have relaxed their standards, including the call to silence.

A PICTURE OF
SILENCE

THE TRAPPIST MONKS

Those Trappists who *do* still adhere to the traditional standards live in absolute silence—including while eating, sleeping, and working. They concentrate on prayer, reading, and working with their hands. In this way, they fulfill what they believe is their calling to grow closer to God in everything they do.

SILENCE

RESPONDING TO GOD

Spend some time in silence. Eliminate as much noise as possible, and concentrate on listening to God. Ask God to speak to you. Write down everything you hear God saying to you.

SILENCE

hose sounds be noise, music, or words."—Dallas Willard

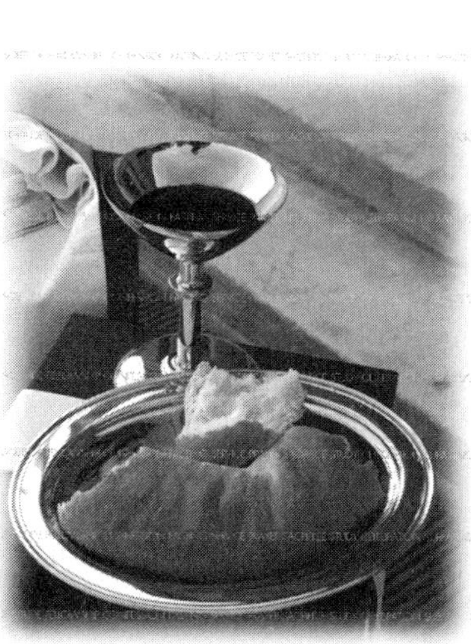